LOVE AND OBSTRUCTION IN MARRIAGE

THE MIRAGE OF LGBTQ RIGHTS

SANKALP MIRANI

NEED FOR SEXUAL AND REPRODUCTIVE HEALTH CARE FOR LGBTQ PEOPLE

Abstract

As we move ahead of 21st century we need to obliterate the transsexual victimization and reconceive to remove the social stigma attached to them. With this present article the author wishes to sensitize the reader with the persistent need for sexual and reproductive health care for the transvestite and create awareness in the society to uphold the issue and speak freely. The author has also tried to strike the contention on the above subject with respect to the Indian law and other laws of the country , here USA. I wish my readers will concur with this contemplation. Happy Reading!

Introduction

All people, including those who draw a parallel with themselves as gay, lesbian, bisexual, transgender and queer (LGBTQ), need sexual and reproductive health care. LGBTQ health problems and sexual and reproductive health care are inextricably linked, as both involve individual independence in their intimate decisions. Unfortunately, the health care system in the United States has historically failed and essentially continues to fail in the LGBTQ community, as LGBTQ people experience significant differences in sexual and reproductive health care and worse health outcomes than the general public.

Historical background

These differences are due to the past series of restrictions on the health care system, including the segregation of health services, provider discrimination and insurance issues, all of which may be exacerbated by racism and racial oppression.

Status quo on Sexual and Reproductive Health Needs

Sexual and reproductive health care services are an integral part of the overall picture of health care for LGBTQ people. In particular, all people who are able to get pregnant — which may include aggressive women, men who are gay, and people who are not binary — may need full-time pregnancy, family planning, and abortion care.A Guttmacher study estimates that a few hundred transgender and non-bisexual people have had abortions nationally in 2017, particularly in institutions that do not provide transgender-based health care.

Differences experienced by LGBTQ in Sexual and Reproductive Healthcare

LGBTQ patients experience differences in sexual and reproductive health care and outcomes. Recent research suggests that non-pregnant women (excluding lesbians) are more likely to have unintended partners with unintended pregnancies, pregnancies under the age of 20 or abortions, findings that may raise structural barriers to contraception and pregnancy. The need for LGBTQ-inclusive comprehensive sex education. Studies have shown that homosexual women and women are less likely to be exposed to sexually transmitted diseases, a view that is associated with reduced use of contraceptives.

These differences in attitudes and practices regarding sexual and reproductive health services can lead LGBTQ people to have fewer diagnoses and treatments than their direct counterparts.

The COVID-19 epidemic could exacerbate the differences that LGBTQ people are already experiencing. A recent Guttmacher study found that 46% of queer women reported an epidemic-related delay or cancellation of contraception or other sexual and

HIV, access to general health care comes with additional barriers such as stigma during dental care, over-protective equipment and unnecessary referrals to professional services.

The Supreme Court has confirmed the equality of alternatives to NALSA vs. Union of India in 2014.38 recognizes the right to self-determination without regard to SRS once other mechanisms that ensure gender, imposing the protection and welfare of the state,

Suggestions

Fortunately, sexual and reproductive health care providers can help and help address these barriers, taking steps to make complementary, life-saving reproductive health care a reality for millions of LGBTQ people across the country.

Organizations working in the health care sector in particular can work deliberately to ensure that their programs are inclusive - that is, people who are exposed to any risk due to their programs and decisions that affect people are not taken without their representation.

OPINION

For LGBTQ people necessity is for infertility care and abetted reproductive automated mechanism , and transvestite women and men may need fertility services. In addition, LGBTQ people may need testing and treatment for STIs and HIV; mammograms, Pap smears and other cervical cancer-related services; testing and support for those close to them and sexual violence; and gender reassurance services.

Conclusion

reproductive health care compared to 31% of straight women.

Mental health of LGBTQ

People who are sexually active and often have higher rates of mental illness than other people. Anxiety, substance abuse and suicidal thoughts were a common part of their experience. One study found that 70% of men who have sex with men (MSM) and 91% of transgender people suffer from depression, alcoholism and frequent victims of violence.

India on the Sexual health of LGBTQ

While a few provinces like Tamil Nadu have made arrangements to provide free SRS services for women shifting, no national policy equally perfect, either access to these services for transgender men in provinces where women are transgender provision of free services.

Sex Reassignment Surgery (SRS) and other gender-based procedures such as Endocrine therapy, some of the less under-discussed issues related to the lower population down to formal priorities, which are crucial to the overall well-being of the ever-changing population

In India, MSM has a human immunodeficiency virus (HIV) of 4.3% while for most people it is 0.3%. However, there are many barriers to MSM testing, including stigma and high testing costs. When it comes to transgender people, about two thirds do not have access to treatment for sexually transmitted infections (STDs).

Although 7.2% of transgender people are living with HIV, only 59% have been referred for testing, and 33% have been offered counseling on treatment options. In fact, for anyone living with

LGBTQ people need and deserve the best sexual and reproductive care. Those who identify themselves as LGBTQ are not monolithic people, and people in that community have different needs, experience with barriers and levels of access to care.

Although issues of discrimination in accessing health care are systematic and require government intervention to address them, there is much that society can do.

Involvement should be part of a business story or program proposal. care must be taken to expand the terms 'gender', 'women' and 'men' to include transgender and non-binary identities. In addition, common perceptions about families and relationships should be avoided as people from these communities often leave their birth families and blood relationships and have a 'chosen' family and the system should not give them authority.

LGBTQIA+ Rights

The idea of human rights rests on the central premise that all humans are equal. It follows that all humans have dignity and all humans should be treated as equal. Anything that undermines that dignity is a violation, for it violates the principle of equality and paves the way for discrimination.

The human rights of lesbian, gay, bisexual, transgender and intersex people (LGBTI) are coming into sharper focus around the world, with important advances in many countries in recent years, including the adoption of new legal protections. The preamble to the Indian Constitution mandates justice — social, economic, and political equality of status — for all. The right of equality before the law and equal protection under the law is guaranteed in Articles 14 and 21 of the Constitution. In April 2014, the Supreme Court of India ruled in NALSA vs Union of India that the rights and freedoms of transgender people in India were protected under the Constitution; in September 2018, the Supreme Court also decriminalized adult consensual same-sex relationships in the Section 377 judgment review. These judgments are considered a landmark both in terms of their expansive reading of constitutional rights and in empowering LGBT persons. Both judgments mark an important moment for LGBT rights that not only reversed a relic of British imperial rule but also ordered that LGBT Indians be accorded all the protections of their constitution. This was a welcome victory, but it does not necessarily mean that LGBT people in India are fully free or perceived as equal among their fellow citizens. It underscores how much work remains to be done in India and the rest of the world to overturn antiquated and repressive anti-gay laws.

In the Indian context, we cannot stand by as people from the Hijra communities are mocked and ostracized. As trans people reliant on begging and sex work are harassed by the cops, harassed by "civil society" and shunned by the "respectable" parts of the community.

An anecdote to share - last year during Trans Day of Remembrance, a memorial gathering took place a few days after pride. The same street that was crowded with cheering people, now lay practically empty. It was a handful of trans people. It was them, and photos of trans women and men who had died. It is the most heartbreaking kind of loneliness to realize that your existence will be tinged with violence just because of who you are. They started to cry and that's when they started hugging each other - almost shielding from photographers that circled the gathering like vultures. "We will NOT give them sad tranny photos" maybe this is what they whispered fiercely as they helped wipe tears. And THAT is a sentiment that will stay with them forever.

As trans people, their lives are forever under scrutiny. Everyone wants to know about "The Struggles" as though they can be saved by being consumed. They ain't a sob story. Trans people aren't your grief porn. They can be seen in the only better way - beautifully.

Right after Pride, the Trans Bill of Protection was passed in the Rajya Sabha. Delhi Pride this year was super political - which, despite what some gross people claim - is an extremely good thing. Pride has and will always be political. It's a protest, it's a show of strength and solidarity.

And they are asking for some of that same solidarity and strength throughout. Sexual assault and violence against trans women carries a ridiculously lax sentence - six months to two years. Let this sink in. It is an awful, evil way of creating a state sponsored divide between cis women and trans women. They're being told that being trans means being less than, therefore crimes committed against them carry a reduced sentence.

There is so much wrong with this bill that I will run out of words trying to break it down.

The passing of this bill makes life even harder for trans folk; as if being trans isn't already an alienating enough experience. The amount of gatekeeping this bill proposes is heinous. The original eight stripe flag created by Baker used two shades of blue - Turquoise to represent Magic and Art; and Indigo to represent Serenity. However after the pink stripe was dropped due to the difficulty in mass-producing hot pink fabric (a cultural loss if you ask me), the rainbow flag underwent another notable transformation.

In 1979, the organisers of the San Francisco pride decided to split the flag in two in order to decorate the two sides of the parade route. This meant that they needed a flag with an even number of stripes.

So Turqoise and Indigo were dropped and ROYAL BLUE was instead used to denote HARMONY; creating the six stripe flag we know today.

The 2018 Social Justice Pride Flag designed by Moulee added a chevron composed of red, blue and black - wherein the Blue represented the Ambedkarite movement and black representing the self respect movement.

Before the creation of the rainbow flag, the Pink Triangle was used as a symbol for the LGBT movement. The Pink Triangle came from a pretty dark time for queer folk. It was created and used by the Nazis to identify and stigmatise queer people.

The ORANGE in the flag represents HEALING.

Healing from a history of stigma and oppression. Each of the colors of the rainbow flag represent something. The original flag came about when Gilbert Baker; an openly gay activist met Harvey Milk and was challenged by Milk to come up with a symbol of pride for the LGBTQ community. Fun fact: In 2018, the Social Justice Pride Flag was released at the Chennai Queer LitFest. Designed by Chennai based activist Moulee. The design incorporates elements representing the Self Respect Movement, the anti-caste movement and leftist ideology. In that iteration of the rainbow flag, Red represents left values.

also worry that today's verdict might trigger a flurry of state legislations, and perhaps national ones too, that are blatantly anti-gay. For example, same-sex marriage and adoption may well be outlawed. In a country where 11 states have independently banned sex education in schools, it is very possible that acts similar to Section 28 in the UK might be enacted. Perhaps I am being overly pessimistic. But having grown up in conservative India where sexuality in general is a big taboo, and having been repeatedly told that homosexuality is abnormal and disgusting, I cannot help but wonder if things really have changed that much. It is easy, and comforting to believe so, but not necessarily true.

The real problem is still the stigma attached, especially outside big cities, said Ritu Dalmia, one of India's best-known chefs, who lives with her girlfriend in New Delhi. Change particularly needs to happen in rural India, she said in an e-mail message Thursday afternoon. I have met women who were forced to sleep with men so that they could be 'cured' of homosexuality, she said. Today is a historical moment where at least some tiny steps have been taken, but there is still a very, very long road ahead, she said.

Hoping that homosexuality remains legal for good, the most important task ahead is to educate the public and raise public awareness about sexual minorities. Sure, popular culture might help. But gay rights activists need the support of the national and state governments, which need to take a secular, long-term outlook, and invest the necessary resources. Unfortunately, where that kind of support is often considered political suicide, achieving equality will take a long time. Today's verdict is just the first step in the right direction.

The Evil West argument is pretty flimsy when it comes to homosexuality and gay rights in India. Here are a few reasons why:

1) Homosexuality has existed throu

ghout human history, all across the world. It has nothing to do with East, West, North, South or any other arbitrary distinctions that we humans invent.

2) Western countries like to oppress homosexuals, too. The West has no shortage of Moral Police types, who spend their lives trying to dictate how others should live.

3) Non-Western countries have embraced gay rights. It would be easier for a gay couple to get married in Nepal right now than in most parts of the United States.

4) In India, it was the British who criminalized homosexuality, not the Indians.

5) Equality and basic human rights are not exclusively Western principles.

India is a vast and diverse country and attitudes towards this subject and experiences of LGBTI individuals vary vastly. The disparity between urban and rural India, language, caste, class, and gender add further complexities to understanding this topic more fully. But what we do know is that India's LGBT citizens are not a "minuscule minority". They have a voice that is strong and refuses to be silent any longer in their efforts to reclaim equality.

Despite homosexuality been decriminalised, the laws in India still remain hostile and prejudicial towards the LGBT community in several ways.The reason behind this is that there exists an enormous gap between the legislative and the judicial development of LGBT laws in India. So, though the Supreme Court of India through the landmark judgements of National Legal Services Authority v. Union of India, Navtej Singh johar v. UOI, and Justice K.S.Puttaswamy v. Union of India (Puttaswamy) has laid the groundwork to confer upon the queer and non-binary community a bundle of basic human rights, but the legislature has failed to keep up with the recent developments.

So essentially speaking, the same-sex couples now have the legal right to cohabit and conduct their personal affairs without any fear of persecution but are still denied equality of treatment in various aspects. Thus, it is imperative to take the conversation forward and talk about the various laws that continue to discriminate against the LGBT+ persons. It includes anti-discriminatory laws such as no recognition of same-sex marriages, no rights for adoption, surrogacy etc.

So, the fight for equality continues as there is a long battle waiting ahead, swarmed with numerous difficulties given that the LGBTQ+ community remains closed off to civil rights. GBT workplace survey of 2016 showed that more than 40% of LGBT people in India have faced harassment at their workplace because of their gender/ sexual identity. Many LGBT people often have to hide their sexual identities because of the fear of potential discrimination or losing their jobs. Therefore the access to employment and discrimination at the workplace continues to pose a challenge for the LGBTQIA+ community.

Transgender people are the worst sufferers

i) Unorganised/ Informal Sector

This situation gets even more depressing in the case of transgender people who often have low levels of literacy, poor access to education and vocational training, and face a much more violent form of discrimination at the workplace. Thus having no other alternative the transgender people often resort to begging or sex work wherein they are disproportionately targeted by the enforcement agencies and are often booked under Immoral

Trafficking Act (1956) and anti-beggary laws.

ii) Instances of workplace discrimination

There have been several instances of workplace discrimination against the transgender people all across the country. One of the publicised cases in this regard is the case of Manish Kumar Giri Alias Sabi Giri Vs Union Of India And Ors.

In the instant case, Sabi Giri, (was earlier a boy named Manish Kumar Gir) who suffered from the Gender dysmorphia and when underwent a sex change operation was dismissed from the navy. Military in defence said that the present rules and regulations do not allow the sailor's continued employment in the navy owing to his altered gender status.

The case was argued in Delhi High court wherein the court suggested the Navy find an alternative job for Giri. Thus despite having no proof of Sabi not being able to do her job after her sex reassignment surgery she was thrown out of her job and was rather offered a job as a data entry operator. Apart from this, the petitioner also testified against the discrimination meted out to her during the course of her employment, highlighting the dark truths about work-place discrimination and the lack of awareness on the issue of transgender rights.

However, it is also important to mention here that the Equal Remunerations Act, 1956 prohibits discrimination between men and women at the stage of recruitment but makes such exceptions in the case of military service where such discrimination is permitted but still the removal of the sailor only on the basis of gender identity is arbitrary, discriminatory and illegal.

Similarly, in the cases of Jacqueline Mary V. Superintendent of police, G.Nagalakshmi V. Director General of Police where the petitioners identifying as females were removed from their posts on the ground that upon medical examination it was found that they had intersex variations hence can't hold the post that was reserved only for females.

Although the court ruled in favour of the petitioners in all the above-mentioned cases these incidents of discrimination reflects gross inequality and do not conform with the NALSA ruling. Therefore, it is submitted that this will keep on continuing until the employment laws are not amended to be inclusive of people falling outside the gender binary.

In India we have our own atrocities to deal with. Conversion therapy has been the cause of death for so many queer kids. Trans women and men are still fighting for the same standing as cis folk. Queer people are still just used for our optics and aesthetics - when its trendy, when it is cool, when it is convenient. But it isn't all for naught. They have come really far. As a society they are becoming more inclusive. As we hurtle toward a future that is scary and uncertain, you'll should be trying to channel power by reminding yourself that you as queer folk have ALWAYS been marching toward a future that is scary and uncertain. But you have done it with grace, aplomb and most importantly - color.

The Canadian Supreme Court endorsed the notion of a disparate impact

where an action has a disproportionate impact on a class of persons. In

Andrews v. Law Society of British Columbia95

, the Court noted:

"Discrimination is a distinction which, whether intentional or not but based on grounds relating to personal characteristics of the individual or group, has an effect which imposes disadvantages not imposed upon others or which withholds or limits access to advantages available to other members of society. Distinctions based on personal characteristics attributed to an individual solely on the basis of association with a group will rarely escape the charge of discrimination, while those based on an individual's merits and capacities will rarely be so classed." (Emphasis supplied) "Cultural homophobia thus discourages social behavior that appears to threaten the stability of heterosexual gender roles. These dual normative standards of social and sexual behavior construct the image of a gay man as abnormal because he deviates from the masculine gender role by subjecting himself in the sexual act to another man."

In 2018, in the landmark decision of Navtej Singh Johar v. Union of India, the Supreme Court of India decriminalised consensual homosexual intercourse by reading down Section 377 of the Indian Penal Code and excluding consensual homosexual sex between adults from its

Multinational research firm Ipsos released report on LGBT+ Pride 2021 Global Survey conducted between April 23 and May 7, 2021. The findings show that 2% of the surveyed online Indian population identify as other than male or female, these include transgender, non-binary, non-conforming, gender-fluid and others. In regards to the sexual orientation, the report shows that 3% of the surveyed Indian population identify as homosexual (Including gay and lesbian), 9% identify as bisexual, 1% identify as pansexual and 2% identify as asexual. Totally, 17% identify as not heterosexual (excluding 'do not know', and 'prefer not to answer').

National Legal Services Authority v. Union of India, Navtej Singh johar v. UOI, and Justice K.S.Puttaswamy v. Union of India (Puttaswamy)

In regards to the sexual orientation, the report shows that 3% of the surveyed Indian population identify as homosexual (Including gay and lesbian), 9% identify as bisexual, 1% identify as pansexual and 2% identify as asexual.

Multinational research firm Ipsos released report on LGBT+ Pride 2021 Global Survey conducted between April 23 and May 7, 2021. The findings show that 2% of the surveyed online Indian population identify as other than male or female, these include transgender, non-binary, non-conforming, gender-fluid and others. In regards to the sexual orientation, the report shows that 3% of the surveyed Indian population identify as homosexual (Including gay and lesbian), 9% identify as bisexual, 1% identify as pansexual and 2% identify as asexual. Totally, 17% identify as not heterosexual (excluding 'do not know', and 'prefer not to answer').

In 2011, a Haryana court granted legal recognition to a same-sex marriage involving two women.[6] After marrying, the couple began to receive threats from friends and relatives in their village. The couple eventually won family approval.

Their lawyer said the court had served notice on 14 of Veena's relatives and villagers who had threatened them with "dire consequences". Haryana has been the centre of widespread protests by villagers who believe their village councils or khaps should be allowed to impose their own punishments on those who disobey their rulings or break local traditions – mainly honour killings of those who marry within their own gotra or sub-caste, regarded in the state as akin to incest. Deputy Commissioner of Police Dr. Abhe Singh told The Daily Telegraph: "The couple has been shifted to a safe house and we have provided adequate security to them on the court orders. The security is provided on the basis of threat perception and in this case the couple feared that their families might be against the relationship."

In October 2017, a group of citizens proposed a draft of a new Uniform Civil Code that would legalise same-sex marriage to the Law Commission of India.

It defines marriage as "the legal union as prescribed under this Act of a man with a woman, a man with another man, a woman with another woman a transgender with another transgender or a transgender with a man or a woman. All married couples in partnership entitled to adopt a child. Sexual orientation of the married couple or the partners not to be a bar to their right to adoption. Non-heterosexual couples will be equally entitled to adopt a child".[

On 12 June 2020, the Uttarakhand High Court acknowledged that while same-sex marriage may not be legal, cohabitation and "live-in relationships" are protected by the law.

In response to a petition filed in the Delhi High Court by a same sex couple to legalise gay marriage, Solicitor General Tushar Mehta representing the Indian Government affirmed that same sex marriage is against Indian culture, showing the government's flip-flopping approach to the issue.

The United States has witnessed a remarkable shift in LGBTQ rights and visibility in the 50 years since the Stonewall uprising — and in just the last few years, LGBTQ people have won the right to marry, have hit a record high in representation on television and have seen the first openly gay major presidential candidate begin his campaign.

But the path of LGBTQ rights in America has not been a simple one. And just as advocates fought their battle American culture, they also did so in the courts, including the U.S. Supreme Court. Over the last half a century, the court first denied and then affirmed that LGBTQ people have the right to consensual sex, and then the right to marry whom they choose.

One, Inc. v. Olesen (1958)

One of the first Supreme Court cases to consider LGBTQ rights concerned freedom of speech.

In 1953, a publisher associated with the Los Angeles chapter of the Mattachine Society, one of the country's first "homophile" groups, released something unique for its time: ONE: The Homosexual Magazine. The magazine, which is considered by One Archives Foundation to be America's first widely-distributed magazine for gay readers, included articles, editorials, short stories and other content. Not long after publication began, its August and October editions were seized by the Los Angeles postal authorities. Authorities argued that the publication violated obscenity laws.

In its decision, the Supreme Court tossed out a lower court's ruling, and established that material aimed at a gay audience was not inherently obscene. The decision validated that people had the right to publish LGBTQ media.

Baker v. Nelson (1972)

The Supreme Court considered the issue of marriage equality for the first time in 1972.

The case was sparked when a young Minneapolis couple, Richard John Baker and James Michael McConnell, wanted to get married. The couple was reportedly so determined that Baker enrolled in law school to figure out a way how the two could legally wed, according to the New York Times. However, the couple's effort seemed to fail when the Supreme Court decided to dismiss the case "for want of a substantial federal question." The case did not end up changing much for people in Baker and McConnell's situation.

Ultimately, the couple got married anyway by obtaining a marriage license in a different Minnesota county in 1971. Baker changed his name to Pat Lyn McConnell to obtain the certificate.

The pastor who married them, Roger Lynn, told the Times in 2015 that he considers them to be "one of my more successful marriages" because they were still happy and love each other. A Minnesota judge ruled that the couple's marriage is valid in 2018.

Bowers v. Hardwick (1986)

The LGBTQ rights movement was dealt a major blow when the court decided to uphold a Georgia sodomy law in 1986.

The subject of the case, Michael Hardwick, had been caught by a Georgia police officer in 1982 having oral sex with another man. The Supreme Court held in a 5-4 ruling, with an opinion by Justice Byron White, that the 14th Amendment's promise of due process doesn't prevent states from criminalizing private, consensual sex between people of the same sex. "Against a background in which many states have criminalized sodomy and still do," White said in the opinion, "to claim that a right to engage in such conduct is 'deeply rooted in this Nation's history and tradition' or 'implicit in the concept of ordered liberty' is, at best, facetious."

Karen Loewy, senior counsel Lambda Legal, which fights for LGBTQ legal rights, tells TIME that Court made a special effort to make clear that the case applied to LGBTQ people, despite the fact that the law didn't refer to the genders of the people involved.

"The court went out of its way to make clear that gay people could be criminalized under these provisions, and there was nothing wrong with that. The court actually turned it into an inquiry about same-sex intimacy where the statute wasn't even that specific," Loewy said.

"It really labeled LGBTQ people as criminals in every sense. Employers would fire people and say, well... it has nothing to do with who you are. It has to do with the fact that you're a criminal."

Robin Maril, associate legal director of the Human Rights Campaign, notes that the conversation about LGBTQ people during that period was shaped by the AIDS epidemic. Many people who feared the then-mysterious disease were "hyper-focused" on the idea that gay men were promiscuous and saw

HIV-positive people as "sort of getting what they deserved," says Maril. "I think AIDs brought out the worst in America."

Hardwick died from complications from AIDS in 1991, and one of his attorneys, Kathleen Wilde said that he had been "very bitter" about the case's outcome, according to the New York Times.

Romer v. Evans (1996)

In this decision, the Supreme Court ruled that laws couldn't single out LGBTQ people to take away their rights.

The case revolved around an amendment to a Colorado law, which banned cities from passing anti-discrimination laws that would protect gay and bisexual people. In a 6-3 decision, Court ruled that the law didn't adhere to the 14th Amendment's equal protection clause, because of how it singled out a certain group. "Even if, as the state contends, homosexuals can find protection in laws and policies of general application," Justice Anthony Kennedy said in the majority opinion, "[the Colorado law] goes well beyond merely depriving them of special rights. It imposes a broad disability upon those persons alone, forbidding them, but no others, to seek specific legal protection."

As Loewy explains, "In Romer, the Supreme Court recognized for the first time that carving LGBTQ people out of protections that everybody else could have access to violated equal protection."

Boy Scouts of America v. Dale (1996)

The same year the court found that laws couldn't single out LGBTQ people, the Supreme Court also considered whether a private organization could single them out with specific rules — and found in favor of that organization.

In 1990, the Boy Scouts of America decided to expel James Dale, an assistant scoutmaster and Eagle Scout, after he was identified in a newspaper as a leader of Rutgers University's Lesbian/Gay Alliance. The New Jersey Supreme Court initially found for Dale on the grounds that the Scouts had violated the state's anti-discrimination law, but that decision was overruled in a 5-4 decision by the Supreme Court. The Court found that forcing the Scouts to readmit Dale would violate their First Amendment right to freedom of association.

"The Boy Scouts asserts that homosexual conduct is inconsistent with the values embodied in the Scout Oath and Law, particularly those represented by the terms 'morally straight' and 'clean,' and that the organization does not want to promote homosexual conduct as a legitimate form of behavior. The Court gives deference to the Boy Scouts' assertions regarding the nature of its expression," Justice William Rehnquist said in the Court's opinion.

"It wasn't until 2013 that the group decided to end its ban on gay children as members, but still continued its ban on gay adult leaders," Dale wrote in a 2015 opinion piece in TIME. "This initiative was wrong in many ways: It was great that they weren't excluding young members, but it was wrong to tell someone that you can be gay when you're a child, but you're immoral as an adult. That's a horrifyingly destructive and damaging thing to say to anyone, especially a young person."

Lawrence v. Texas (2003)

The Court ultimately eliminated sodomy laws in 2003, overruling Bowers v. Hardwick with a vote of 6-3.

Justice Kennedy delivered the opinion, saying that the due process clause of the fourteenth amendment gave the petitioners "the full right to engage in private conduct without government intervention... The Texas statute furthers no legitimate state interest which can justify its intrusion into the individual's personal and private life."

Loewy notes that her organization fought for this decision, and helped to popularize the idea that "public ideas about morality cannot justify infringing people's constitutional rights." Loewy says that this was an essential case because "the court really recognized that LGBTQ people are entitled to constitutional protections for intimate conduct. For private, consensual, intimate conduct."

United States v. Windsor (2013)

This case was one of the major precursors to marriage equality. The Court decided to eliminate the portion of the Defense of Marriage Act (DOMA) of 1996 that defined marriage as a "legal union between one man and one woman as husband and wife."

The case considered the situation of Edith Windsor and Thea Spyer, who were married in Canada before moving to New York, a state that recognized their marriage. After Spyer passed away, Windsor's attempted to claim a tax exemption for surviving spouses — only to be blocked by DOMA. In a 5-4 vote, Supreme Court ruled that DOMA violates due process and equal protection principles, and ordered the United States to refund Windsor's taxes.

"DOMA's principal effect is to identify a subset of state-sanctioned marriages and make them unequal. The principal purpose is to impose inequality, not for other reasons like governmental efficiency," said Justice Kennedy in the opinion.

Obergefell v Hodges (2015)

A group of 14 same-sex couples and two men whose partners were deceased joined together and won one of the LGBTQ rights movement's biggest victories: marriage.

In a 5-4 vote, the Supreme Court found for the petitioners, who argued that state officials violated the 14th amendment's equal protection clause by prohibiting them from marrying or not recognizing marriages performed in other states.

"It is demeaning to lock same-sex couples out of a central institution of the Nation's society, for they too may aspire to the transcendent purposes of marriage," Justice Kennedy said in the Court's opinion.

The court also extended them the benefits guaranteed to opposite-sex married couples. Maril argues that while she personally values the emotional aspect of matrimony, getting married in the United States is considered to be a legal status.

"At the end of the day, it's social security benefits, it's survivor benefits. It's healthcare. It's super unromantic," Maril says.

Loewy argues that this decision also had a profound cultural impact, because it gave LGBTQ people a "common language" with straight people.

Masterpiece Cakeshop, Ltd. v. Colorado Civil Rights Commission (2018)

Although by 2018 LGBTQ people could marry, the Supreme Court found that a baker was not required to make wedding cakes for same-sex marriages.

In a 7-2 decision, the Supreme Court found for Colorado baker Jack Phillips, who had refused to make a gay couple a wedding cake on religious grounds. Phillips argued that baking cakes requires his "artistic skills" and being forced to bake the cake would have infringed upon his freedom of speech and his rights to practice his religion.

However, the Court's argument in favor of Phillips hinged upon the state's "impermissible hostility toward his sincere religious beliefs.," noting that a commissioner compared Phillips' religious beliefs to defending slavery or the Holocaust.

"The government cannot pass judgment upon or presuppose the illegitimacy of religious beliefs and practices. The state's interest could have been weighed against Phillips' sincere religious objections in a way consistent with the requisite religious neutrality," Justice Kennedy said in the opinion.

Contents